BIG HISTORY
TIMELINE
STICKERBOOK

SPACE

COMET BOMBARDMENT
Storms of comets rain down on the Earth's surface, bringing with them molecules such as water and amino acids that may help seed life.

JIGSAW E...
Like giant jigsa...
the Earth's co...
crusts gradually f...
the planet's surfa...
mountains when...

SK...

THE SUN
The Sun is created out of the scattered remains of one or more previous stars. The material collapses and ignites.

FORMATION OF EARTH
Floating particles of rock, dust and gas collide and stick together to form the early Earth.

TORRENTIAL RAINS
Torrential rains cause sea levels to rise. The sky is blood red due to high levels of carbon dioxide in the air.

THE MILKY WAY
Our galaxy forms about 500 million years after the Big Bang.

OXYGEN
Cyanobacteria live on the surfaces of layered rocks that jut out of the seas. They give off oxygen gas as waste.

TRILOB...
Primitive arth...
among the firs...
able to see...
underw...

HALLUCIGE...
A kind of sea...
appears with...
armor on its...

BACTERIA
The first signs of life emerge in the seas. Simple bacteria dominate life on Earth for at least two billion years.

THE BIG BANG
A colossal explosion of infinite energy triggers the birth of our universe.

350 MILLION YEARS AGO

200 MILLION YEARS AGO

90 MILLION YEARS AGO

45 MILLIC YEAR AGO

FLYING HIGH
Griffinflies grow to the size of pigeons, possibly because of higher levels of oxygen in the air.

PTERODACTYLS
Some have wingspans that extend up to 40-feet wide.

PROTEROCTOPUS
An ancestor of the octopus emerges in the seas.

MAMMALS
Mammals survive the mass extinction thanks to their sma size, unfussy eating habits, an skills at living in the dark.

DUNKLEOSTEUS
This 30-foot-long fish has fierce plate-like jaws that snap open in less than a fiftieth of a second, sucking up nearby prey.

SEA

SEA SCORPIONS
Predators with poisonous stings make life in the seas nasty, brutish and short.

LEPIDODENDRON
90-foot-high trees dominate the landscape.

DIPLODOCUS
A 90-foot-long sauropod, one of the largest ever land animals.

METEORITE STRIKE
A 6-mile-wide rock from outer space collides with the Earth causing a global environmental catastrophe that kills off the land-based dinosaurs.

LAND

DIMETRODON
The "sail" on mammal-like *Dimetrodon*'s back may have been used to cool and heat its body.

TYRANNOSAURUS REX
A highly aggressive meat-eating dinosaur.

RTH
pieces,
tinental
at around
, creating
ey collide.

Y

TES
opods are
creatures
clearly
ter.

IA
orm
piky
ack.

20 MILLION YEARS AGO

2 MILLION YEARS AGO

150 THOUSAND YEARS AGO

7 THOUSAND YEARS BC

WHALES
Descendants of hoofed land animals return to the seas and evolve into dolphins and whales.

BIRDS FLY SOUTH
Birds adapt to the ice ages by migrating around the world, seeking the best conditions for breeding and feeding.

WOOLLY MAMMOTHS
Some mammals grow exceptionally large during the ice ages. Extra body fat helps keep them warm.

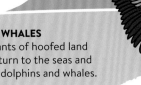

PLIOHIPPUS
Ancestors of today's horses evolve in North America, growing larger as the climate dries out.

MASTODON
A mixture of overhunting and climate change causes a mass extinction of mammals in the Americas.

NEANDERTHALS
Another species of humans populates Europe and Africa with brains as large, if not larger, than those of humans today.

HOMO ERECTUS
Upright humans populate Africa, Europe and Asia where they make tools, weapons and learn how to light and control fire.

HOMO SAPIENS
Homo sapiens evolve in Africa and migrate into Europe and Asia eventually reaching Australia and the Americas.

PRIMATES
Some primates remain in Africa while others migrate to the Americas.

AUSTRALOPITHECUS
Human ancestors walk on two feet. Their head size is about 30 cubic inches.

STONE AGE

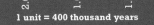

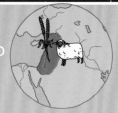

3 THOUSAND YEARS BC

1500 YEARS BC

1000 YEARS BC

5
Y
1

FIRST FARMERS
People living near fertile river valleys (such as the Nile, Jordan, Indus, Tigris and Euphrates) experiment with farming as a new way of securing a steady food supply.

PADDY FIELDS
Chinese farmers cultivate highly nutritious crops of millet and rice, which boost human populations.

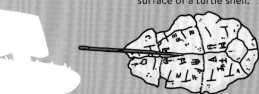

ORACLE BONES
Shang kings of China try to divine the will of the gods by seeing which way the cracks point when a hot rod breaks the surface of a turtle shell.

CONFUCIUS
A court schola
advises kings as
what is morally ri
and wrong.
His works becom
great classics.

ASIA

CHINA

HERBAL TEA
Chinese farmers grow tea and brew the leaves as a drink.

BUDDHA
Indian prince Siddhar
Gautama gains
enlightenment und
a fig tree. He becom
known as the Buddh

SILK MAKING
According to legend, Chinese Empress Leizu discovers the art of silk making when a moth's cocoon unravels in her cup of tea.

INDUS VALLEY
People living in northern India develop an advanced civilization with writing, trade and crafts.

ISRAELITES
Jewish leader Moses leads the Israelites out of Egypt.

TRIREM
Traders from l
develop the
most advanc

Egypt

RIVER NILE
Egyptian civilization reaches its peak of power thanks to the agricultural benefits of the River Nile.

PYRAMIDS
Egyptian ruler Khufu constructs the pyramids of Giza with a labor force of 100,000 farmers. His Great Pyramid becomes the first of the seven wonders of the ancient world.

TROJAN WARS
Bronze and iron weapons, mounted cavalry, wheeled chariots, and growing populations provide the ingredients for a major increase in violence, beginning with the legendary Trojan Wars.

Greece

WRITING
Merchants in the Middle East establish the art of writing to keep account of products they have bought and sold.

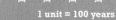

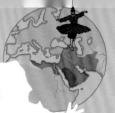
TERRACOTTA ARMY
Chinese emperor Qin Shi Huangdi has an army built out of clay to protect him in the afterlife.

China

PAPER-MAKING
Chinese scholar Cai Lun is credited with inventing a way of making paper out of the mashed bark of mulberry trees.

GUNPOW
Legend says th monks discover t gunpowder whi find a potion to Emperor live

Israel

CLEOPATRA
After the death of Cleopatra, Egypt is absorbed into the Roman Empire.

NORTH AFRICA & MIDDLE EAST

CONSTANTINOPLE
Emperor Justinian I orders the construction of a magnificent basilica in Constantinople.

PERSIAN EMPIRE
Shah Khosrow, Emperor of Persia, builds temples, roads, and canals. He also introduces chess to the Middle East.

HOUSE O
Scholars tra texts and pione optics, medicine, chemistry an

Romans

EUROPE

INVENTIONS
Greek scientists develop expertise in math and geometry. Archimedes invents water pumps and pulleys.

THE ROMANS
The mighty Roman Empire reaches its greatest extent, stretching throughout Europe, the Middle East and North Africa.

ELEPHANT ATTACK
Carthaginian general Hannibal tries to capture Rome after crossing the Alps with a herd of elephants.

NAZCA LINES
Nazca people from Peru make paths in the desert into shapes that they believe can be recognized by their gods.

MAYA
An advanced civilization with writing, math and impressive buildings, including pyramids, emerges in Central America.

SPEARTHROWER OWL
Spearthrower Owl becomes king of Teotihuacan.

Diseas and hu

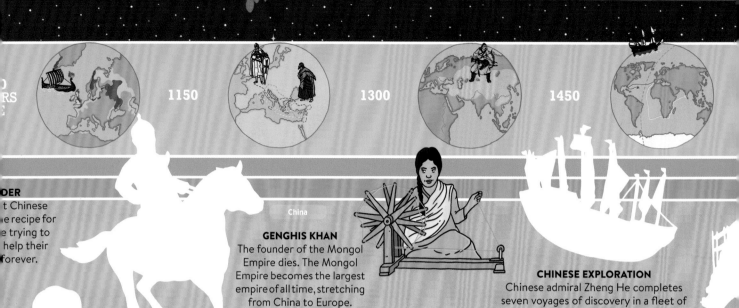

1150   1300   1450

...DER
...t Chinese
...e recipe for
...e trying to
...help their
...forever.

China

GENGHIS KHAN
The founder of the Mongol Empire dies. The Mongol Empire becomes the largest empire of all time, stretching from China to Europe.

CHINESE EXPLORATION
Chinese admiral Zheng He completes seven voyages of discovery in a fleet of enormous ships. He reaches the coast of East Africa.

BLACK DEATH
The Black Death spreads across central Asia. It is carried by fleas that live off rats and kills up to 50 million people across Europe.

FALL OF CONSTANTINOPLE
Ottoman forces capture Constantinople from the Byzantine Greeks. The city is later renamed Istanbul.

...WISDOM
...slate Greek
...r research into
...math, astronomy,
...d geography.

CRUSADES
European countries join forces in a series of attempts to conquer Jerusalem.

CASTLES
Fortifications are built across France, Spain, Italy and England.

Germany

JOUSTING
European knights fight for honor in medieval jousting contests.

PRINTING PRESS
Johannes Gutenberg invents the first moveable-type printing press.

Incas

Aztecs

MANCO CÁPAC
The legendary founder of the Inca dies. He is worshipped as a son of the Sun god Inti.

MACHU PICCHU
Pachacuti, the ninth Inca ruler, builds a magnificent summer palace at Machu Picchu.

THE NEW WORLD
Christopher Columbus leaves Spain in an attempt to find a new sea route to the Far East. He discovers a "New World."

AMERICAS

Pueblos

CHACO CANYON
Ancestral Pueblo people build elaborate complexes in the mountainous regions of New Mexico.

HERNÁN CORTÉS
Spanish Conquistado... Hernán Cortés defea... the Aztecs.

Kingdom of Mali

MANSA MUSA
Mali monarch, Mansa Musa, goes on a pilgrimage to Mecca with 24,000 pounds of gold, some of which he gives to the poor along the way.

Por...
the re...
built
w...

TSETSE FLY
...e-carrying flies attack cattle
...mans, preventing the spread
...f agriculture in Africa.

SUB-SAHARAN A

1000 1020 1040 1060 1080 1100 1120 1140 1160 1180 1200 1220 1240 1260 1280 1300 1320 1340 1360 1380 1400 1420 1440 1460 1480 1500 1510 1520

1 unit = 20 years

1570 GLOBE 1600 1680 1770

China

GREAT WALL OF CHINA
The Ming Emperors of China build a great wall in an attempt to ward off invaders from the north.

India

TAJ MAHAL
Construction of the most famous funerary monument in India is completed by Mughal Emperor Shah Jahan. It is built to house the tomb of his third wife who dies when giving birth to their 14th child.

CHINESE DICTIONARY
47,000 different Chinese characters are published in a massive new dictionary by the Emperor Kangxi.

China

SAFAVIDS
Persian Shah Abbas seizes power in Iran and creates a new dynasty. He transforms the Persian army, hiring experts to train his troops to use firearms.

ZAND DYNASTY
Karim Khan Zand founds the Zand dynasty in Iran, bringing in an era of peace and prosperity.

Ottomans

WILLIAM SHAKESPEARE
The world's most famous playwright writes 38 plays in 23 years.

France

GREAT FIRE
London burns after a fire breaks out on Pudding Lane.

PALACE OF VERSAILLES
The enormous Palace of Versailles symbolizes the vast gap between rich and poor that boils over into revolution in 1789.

Britain

The 13 Colonies

USA

MAYFLOWER
The *Mayflower* sets sail from Plymouth, England to the New World.

DECLARATION OF INDEPENDENCE
On July 4th 1776, the Declaration of Independence is adopted.

SOUT
IND
Sir
cham
and S
ind

VIRGINIA COLONY
John Smith founds the first successful English colony in Jamestown, Virginia.

COFFEE AND SUGAR
Coffee and sugar become the Americas' biggest exports.

T ZIMBABWE
se explorers find
of a giant stone city
en 1000 and 1400
oused as many
000 people.

NIGERIA
Queen Amina dies after ruling Zazzau (Nigeria) for 34 years. She is famous for leading her army in battle throughout her reign.

ZULUS
Shaka Zulu unites his people into a 50,000-strong army.

FRICA

Australia

1550 1560 1570 1580 1590 1600 1610 1620 1630 1640 1650 1660 1670 1680 1690 1700 1710 1720 1730 1740 1750 1760 1770 1780 1790 1800 1810 1820

1 unit = 10 years

1850

1910

1945

THE WRIGHT FLYER
The first heavier-than-air human flight takes off in Kitty Hawk, North Carolina.

MOON LANDING
Neil Armstrong is the first person to walk on the Moon.

OPIUM WARS
British warships destroy Chinese cities up the Yangtze River in protest against Chinese trading bans.

British India

India

MAHATMA GANDHI
Indian leader Mahatma Gandhi protests nonviolently against British rule.

China

CHAIRMAN MAO
The People's Republic of China is founded as a one-party socialist state.

FLORENCE NIGHTINGALE
British nurse Florence Nightingale discovers the importance of hygiene after treating wounded soldiers in the Crimean War. She founds the first school of nursing.

VLADIMIR LENIN
Communist revolutionary Vladimir Lenin leads a Russian revolution and becomes premier of the Soviet Union.

GLOBALIZATION
China becomes the world's biggest manufacturing nation

MOTHER TERESA
A Roman Catholic missionary from Albania receives the Nobel Peace Prize for her work helping the poor and sick in India.

PRIME MINISTER
Margaret Thatcher becomes Britain's first female prime minister.

NAPOLEON
French Emperor Napoleon is defeated by British forces at the Battle of Waterloo.

WORLD WAR I
Archduke Ferdinand of Austria is killed, triggering a four-year world war.

WORLD WAR II
War breaks out in Europe and spreads across the world.

MIDDLE EAST CONFLIC
Following the attacks of 9/11, Allies invade Ira and Afghanistan.

BARACK OBAMA
The U.S. elects Barack Obama, the country's first African American president.

STATUE OF LIBERTY
The French people give a statue to the American people to celebrate liberty.

H AMERICAN EPENDENCE
ón Bolívar ions Central uth American ependence.

HENRY FORD
Henry Ford pioneers mass car production.

MARTIN LUTHER KING JR.
America reels from the assassination of Martin Luther King Jr., leader of a campaign against racial inequality.

THE KING
Elvis Presley dies at Graceland.

SMART PHONES
Smart phones spark a mobile Internet revolution.

NELSON MANDELA
Nelson Mande is freed by F.W de Klerk. Apartheid South Africa is replaced by a new democratic state.

RABBITS
Rabbit populations in Australia reach 500 million causing widespread damage to crops.

AFRICAN INDEPENDENCE
Independence of Ghana from Britain sparks other African countries to break from European rule.

1840 | 1850 | 1860 | 1870 | 1880 | 1890 | 1900 | 1905 | 1910 | 1915 | 1920 | 1925 | 1930 | 1935 | 1940 | 1945 | 1950 | 1955 | 1960 | 1965 | 1970 | 1975 | 1980 | 1985 | 1990 | 1995 | 2000 | 2010

1 unit = 5 years

BIG HISTORY TIMELINE STICKERBOOK

This stickerbook belongs to:

....

....

How to use the Big History Timeline Stickerbook

What on Earth? Stickerbooks tell giant stories using stickers on a timeline.
To make your own Big History stickerbook, unfold the timeline and put
the stickers from the following pages in the correct places.
Once you have finished, carefully tear the timeline along
the perforated edge and stick it up on the wall.

You can also color in our What on Earth? illustration, which you will
find on the other side of this page.

Color in What on Earth!

How many moments from Big History can you find? Can you guess what they are?

Asia

GUNPOWDER

SILK MAKING

GENGHIS KHAN

GLOBALIZATION

INDUS

CHINESE EXPLORATION

HERBAL TEA

CHAIRMAN MAO

CONFUCIUS

CHINESE DICTIONARY

GREAT WALL OF CHINA

MOTHER TERESA

BUDDHA

TERRACOTTA ARMY

PADDY FIELDS

TAJ MAHAL

PAPER-MAKING

OPIUM WARS

MAHATMA GANDHI

Africa, Middle East & Australasia

PERSIAN EMPIRE

HOUSE OF WISDOM

ZULUS

MIDDLE EAST CON
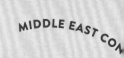

NIGERIA

RIVER NILE

CLEOPATRA

TRIREMES

NELSON MANDELA

PYRAMIDS
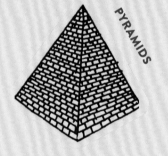

CONSTANTINOPLE

GREAT ZIMBABWE

TSETSE

WRITING

RABBITS

ISRAELITES

MANSA MUSA

FALL OF CONSTANTINOPLE

AFRICAN INDEPENDENCE

ZAN

SAFAVIDS

Natural History & the Stone Age

THE SUN

OXYGEN

PLIOHIPPUS

FLYING HIGH

MAMMALS

WOOLLY MAMMOTHS

TORRENTIAL RA

BACTERIA

HOMO SAPIENS

TRILOBITES

LEPIDODENDRON

DIMETRODON

NEANDERTHALS

FORMATION OF EARTH

DUNKLEOSTEUS

HALLUCIGENIA

WHALES

SEA SCORPIONS

JIGSAW EARTH

FIRST FARMERS

COMET BOMBARDMENT

TYRANNOSAURUS REX

PTERODACTYLS

METEORITE STRIKE

BIRDS FLY SOUTH

AUSTRALOPITHECUS

MASTODON

DIPLODOCUS

PRIMATES

THE MILKY WAY

HOMO ERECTUS

PROTEROCTOPUS

Europe

THE ROMANS

FLORENCE NIGHTINGALE

BLACK DEATH

CRUSADES

TROJAN WARS

ELEPHANT ATTACK

WORLD WAR II

PRINTING PRESS

PRIME MINISTER

WORLD WAR I

JOUSTING

CASTLES

NAPOLEON

WILLIAM SHAKESPEARE

THE NEW WORLD

INVENTIONS

GREAT FIRE

VLADIMIR LENIN

PALACE OF VERSAILLES

Americas

HENRY FORD

COFFEE AND SUGAR

THE KING

NAZCA LINES

SPEARTHROWER OWL

VIRGINIA COLONY

STATUE OF LIBERTY

MANCO CÁPAC

MACHU PICCHU

CHACO CANYON

DECLARATION OF INDEPENDENCE

350 CE GLOBE

THE WRIGHT FLYER

1570 GLOBE

MARTIN LUTHER KING JR.

BARACK OBAMA

SMART PHONES

MAYFLOWER

MOON LANDING

MAYA

SOUTH AMERICAN INDEPENDENCE

HERNÁN CORTÉS

THE STICKERBOOK TIMELINE COLLECTION

OUR TIMELINES COME IN THREE FABULOUS FORMATS:

WALLBOOKS feature a six-foot timeline, plus a newspaper packed with stories, pictures, letters and a quiz. Perfect for everyone aged 6 - 106.

STICKERBOOKS each have around a hundred stickers and a five-foot simplified version of the timeline to stick them on to. Perfect for younger readers.

POSTERBOOKS are gigantic ten-foot versions of the timeline, printed on heavy paper and laminated for extra durability. Perfect for schools.

1. Nature 2. Science 3. Big History

AMERICAN MUSEUM
OF NATURAL HISTORY

Published by What on Earth Publishing Ltd. © 2017 All rights reserved.
ISBN: 978-0-9955766-5-0
PK/Belgrade, Serbia/11/2021

10 9 8 7 6 5 4 3 2

Contact us at info@whatonearthbooks.com or visit whatonearthbooks.com